CONTENTS

A
S
S
E
M
B
L
E

THE AVENGERS ANNUAL is published by Panini Publishing, a division of Panini UK Limited. Mike Riddell, Managing Director. Alan O'Keefe, Managing Editor. Mark Irvine, Production Manager. Marco M. Lupoi, Publishing Director Europe. Editorial: Ed Hammond, Design: Tim Warran-Smith & Will Lucas. Office of publication: Brockbourne House, 77 Mount Ephraim, Tunbridge Wells, Kent TN4 8BS.

£7.99

LONG, LONG AGO...

SUPPER! I DEMAND MY SUPPER!!

OR I SHALL TURN YOU ALL INTO FROGS-- EACH AND EVERY ONE OF YOU!

CAUSING A RUCKUS, MERLIN? TSK, TSK.

PAH! COME FOR ANOTHER GLOAT, HAVE YOU?

NOT STILL UPSET ABOUT THE BELT? COME COME, I'VE BEEN CHANNELLING YOUR MAGIC WITH IT FOR WEEKS NOW. CAN'T WE LET BYGONES BE BYGONES?

YOU CAN'T BEGIN TO CONTROL THAT BELT! IT CONTAINS MORE POWER THAN YOU CAN POSSIBLY IMAGINE!

OH, DON'T THINK POORLY OF ME. WHY, WE'RE TWO SIDES OF THE SAME COIN, YOU AND I.

OF COURSE, WHEN HEADS IS SHOWING, TAILS HAS TO LIE FACE DOWN IN THE DIRT. THAT'S THE THING ABOUT COINS. SO UNFAIR.

TODAY. BERGEN, OKLAHOMA. THE BERGEN WAR MEMORIAL MUSEUM.

OKAY... ANY IDEAS WHAT *THIS* ONE IS?

THAT IS A *BELT BUCKLE*... NO, WAIT. A *CENTERPIECE* FOR A *SHIELD*.

YOU SURE?

NO. NOT REALLY.

SORRY, THOR. I THOUGHT YOU'D BE *GOOD* AT THIS. THESE ARE MAINLY *NORDIC* ARTIFACTS, RIGHT?

THEY ARE *EARTH* ARTIFACTS. AND I AM NOT OF EARTH.

YEAH.

YOU SEEM *SHORT OF TEMPER* TONIGHT, JANE. IS SOMETHING WRONG?

I...I GOT A LETTER FROM MY BROTHER *HAL*, ASKING FOR *MONEY*. HE'S IN A *FIX*... BUT IT'S HIS *OWN FAULT*, *GAMBLING*. AND IT'S NOT LIKE I HAVE IT TO SPARE.

IT'S NOT THE *FIRST* TIME, EITHER. UNTIL NOW I'VE ALWAYS SAID *NO*...

...BUT NOW I'M WONDERING IF THAT WAS THE RIGHT THING TO DO.

WHAT DO *YOU* THINK, THOR?

THOR?

PRESENTING--
TOGETHER AGAIN FOR THE FIRST TIME!--
CAPTAIN AMERICA & THOR in

"ONCE AND FUTURE AVENGERS!"

ROGER LANGRIDGE • **writer**
CHRIS SAMNEE • **artist**
MATTHEW WILSON • colorist   VC's RUS WOOTON • letterer
CHRIS SAMNEE & MATTHEW WILSON • cover
SANA AMANAT & MICHAEL HORWITZ • editors
AXEL ALONSO • editor in chief   JOE QUESADA • chief creative officer
DAN BUCKLEY • publisher   ALAN FINE • executive producer

YOU **YELLED.**

AS DID YOU.

I JUST GOT HERE... **UNEXPECTEDLY.** WHAT'S YOUR **EXCUSE?**

IT...SEEMS WE SHARE A PREDICAMENT. I AM **THOR,** SON OF ODIN.

CAPTAIN AMERICA. YOU...

THOR? REALLY?

REALLY. SO I AM STILL IN **AMERICA...**

SO I'M IN **SCANDINAVIA...**

HOLD ON. **DUCK!**

I THOUGHT I SAW A **GLINT OF LIGHT** THAT SHOULDN'T BE THERE. I WAS **RIGHT.**

AN... **ASSASSIN?**

LOOKS LIKE IT.

AND THAT... IS PROBABLY HIS **QUARRY.**

CONTINUED ON PAGE 13

CAPTAIN AMERICA!

SENTINEL OF LIBERTY!

Transformed by an experimental Super-Soldier Serum into a man at the very peak of human fitness, Steve Rogers is Captain America. During World War 2, he helped the Allied Forces to victory by destroying the evil Red Skull and his HYDRA army.

END OF THE ROAD!

On his final mission, Captain America was forced to make the ultimate sacrifice by ditching the jet he was piloting into the frozen wastes of the Arctic. Buried beneath the ice, it was nearly 70 years before anyone found the crash site.

THE RETURN!

Somehow, the Super-Soldier Serum in his veins kept Rogers in perfect hibernation and he was able to be revived. Now living in a world very different to the one he knew, he awaits the call for when his amazing abilities will be needed once more.

AVENGERS FACT!

His shield is made from a rare energy absorbing metal called Vibranium and is virtually indestructible.

B A M N
R I U U I

Captain America isn't just physically superior to normal people – he's a tactical genius too! Can you match his skills by rearranging these letters to form a new word?

ANSWER

THE MIGHTY THOR™

BEYOND THE STARS!

Thor is not of this world. He actually comes from Asgard, a land far beyond the reach of mortal man with a civilisation much more advanced than our own. He is the son of King Odin, ruler of Asgard, and a brave, courageous warrior.

AVENGERS FACT!

Thor's hammer can control storms, allowing him to fire bolts of lightning or summon howling gales.

EXILED!

As punishment for his arrogance, Thor was recently banished to Earth by King Odin and stripped of his powers. Whilst here, Thor learnt a valuable lesson in humility and managed to return to Asgard just in time to stop his brother from taking over the kingdom.

LOKI'S REVENGE!

Now that Loki has turned his attention to Earth, Thor must once again return to protect our planet from his brother's wicked intentions. Armed with his elemental hammer Mjolnir, he will do all he can to help the Avengers in their plight.

AVENGERS FACT!

Like all Asgardians, Thor possesses superhuman

ORIGINAL

A **B**

C **D** **E**

Only one of these hammers is an exact match to Mjolnir. See if you can work out which one it is!

ALWAYS *WANTED* TO WEAR THIS STUFF...

SO, YOUR MAJESTY...GET A *LOT* OF ASSASSINATION ATTEMPTS, DO YOU?

ALAS, *YES,* CAPTAIN...PART OF THE PRICE ONE PAYS FOR BEING *KING.*

I SEE.

WHAT *BRINGS* YOU OUT HERE, ANYWAY?

YOU JOIN US AT THE END OF THE *GREAT QUEST,* CAPTAIN! AFTER MANY YEARS I, SIR GAWAIN, HAVE FINALLY FOUND THE *GRAIL!*

GRAIL? WHAT, THE *HOLY GRAIL?*

INDEED! ARTHUR AND MERLIN MET ME TWO DAYS AGO TO ESCORT ME HOME IN *SAFETY*...THOUGH, JUDGING BY THOSE *VARLETS* YOU APPREHENDED, I FEAR WORD OF MY SUCCESS HAS *PRECEDED* ME.

BUT...BUT THIS IS *AMAZING!* THOR AND I WERE *BROUGHT* HERE BY A *MAGICAL CUP*...COULD THAT BE THE *GRAIL?* A PLAIN GOBLET MADE OF, WHAT, PEWTER...?

LIKE *THIS* ONE?

OH.

THOSE THINGS ARE AS *COMMON AS MUD,* CAPTAIN. NO, THE GRAIL IS AN ALTOGETHER *FANCIER* AFFAIR. A VESSEL WITH *DEEP SIGNIFICANCE* TO THOSE WHO SHARE OUR FAITH...

"...AND THE MOST *POWERFUL* MYSTICAL ARTIFACT IN *ALL OF CHRISTENDOM!*"

A...A DRAGON! IN THE NAME OF OUR LORD...IS SUCH A THING POSSIBLE?

SIRE...I SUGGEST WE SAVE THE PHILOSOPHY--

T'HWOCK

SCHWIPP

--FOR AFTER THE FUNERAL!

TER-RIFIC.

DON'T DO THAT AG--

CONTINUED ON PAGE 23

Loki™
MASTER OF MISCHIEF

LORD OF LIES!

Even though Loki is Thor's step-brother, the two Asgardians couldn't be less alike. Whereas Thor is a brave, courageous warrior who will fight to the end to help those in need, Loki is a scheming sneak who uses magic and lies to trick his way into getting what he wants.

THE RULE OF LOKI!

Loki hasn't been seen since his failed attempt to banish Thor from Asgard and seize the throne for himself. Now on Earth, he means to create a new empire by enslaving the human race.

UNSTOPPABLE FORCE!

If Loki can find a way to permanently open a gateway to Earth, he could bring through an alien army that will conquer the planet in hours. Only by working together will the Avengers have any hope of stopping his plans to rule the planet.

LOKI'S SCEPTRE!

This powerful and msyterious artifact can be used to mind control people turning them into Loki's obedient slaves. It can also fire devastating energy blasts.

POWER OF THE TESSERACT!

Created by the Asgardians, the Tesseract is an ancient device of unlimited power that somehow ended up on Earth. Over 60 years ago the Red Skull tried to use its cosmic power for his own evil plans but was stopped by Captain America. Since then it has been kept safely hidden away by S.H.I.E.L.D.

MIND GAMES!

Loki's mastery of magic allows him to create incredible life-like illusions to trick his foes.

But when a S.H.I.E.L.D. science team begin experimenting on the Tesseract, Loki is able to use its immense power to transport himself to Earth. Finally free from his exile, he has only one thing on his mind – total global domination!

HAWKEYE

SHARP-SHOOTER!

Agent Clint Barton, better known by his codename Hawkeye, is S.H.I.E.L.D.'s number one sharpshooter. But guns and rifles aren't Clint's thing – he prefers to take on the bad guys with his trademark compound bow!

UNBEATABLE AIM!

Hawkeye's natural accuracy and incredible aim verges on the brink of super human. There's not a single person on the planet, not even an Olympic level archer, who can match his accuracy with a bow and arrow.

AVENGERS FACT!

Even without his bow, Hawkeye is still a match for most opponents thanks to his S.H.I.E.L.D. martial arts training.

TRICK SHOTS!

So that he's always got the right tool for the job, Hawkeye has access to a vast array of special trick arrows, including explosive tipped, flare and armour piercing. His hi-tech quiver automatically rotates and fits the special tips onto the arrow shafts in a matter of seconds.

Take a look at these target an see if you can work out how many points Hawkeye has scored in total

5

15

10

50

20

ANSWER

20

CONTINUED FROM PAGE 19

WHAAAMMM!

OD'S BLOOD! WHAT TRICKERY IS THIS...?

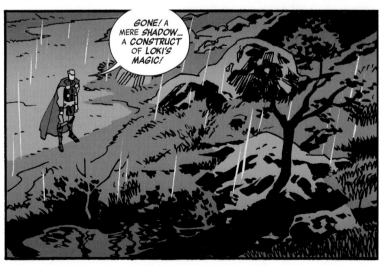

GONE! A MERE *SHADOW*... A *CONSTRUCT* OF *LOKI'S* MAGIC!

THE END

HULK™

ORIGINS!

...hilst working on a way ...recreate the Super-...dier Serum that ...ve Captain America ... powers, brilliant ...entist Bruce Banner ... accidentally ...posed to a ...ngerous blast of ...mma radiation.

MONSTER MUTATION!

...mehow the radiation ...ered his body at a ...llular level. Now, ...en he becomes angry ... stressed Banner ...ansforms into an ...most uncontrollable ...oot-tall, musclebound, ...een-skinned ...onster!

THE HERO INSIDE!

Dubbed the Hulk, Banner's rampaging alter-ego is a force of nature not to be messed with. But with a grave threat facing the Earth, Banner must find a way to help the Avengers by controlling the Hulk and adding his unstoppable power to the fight.

AVENGERS FACT!
As the Hulk gets angrier, he also gets stronger.

AVENGERS FACT!
The Hulk can leap over 300 feet in a single bound.

Take cover, True Believers! The Hulk is on the rampage

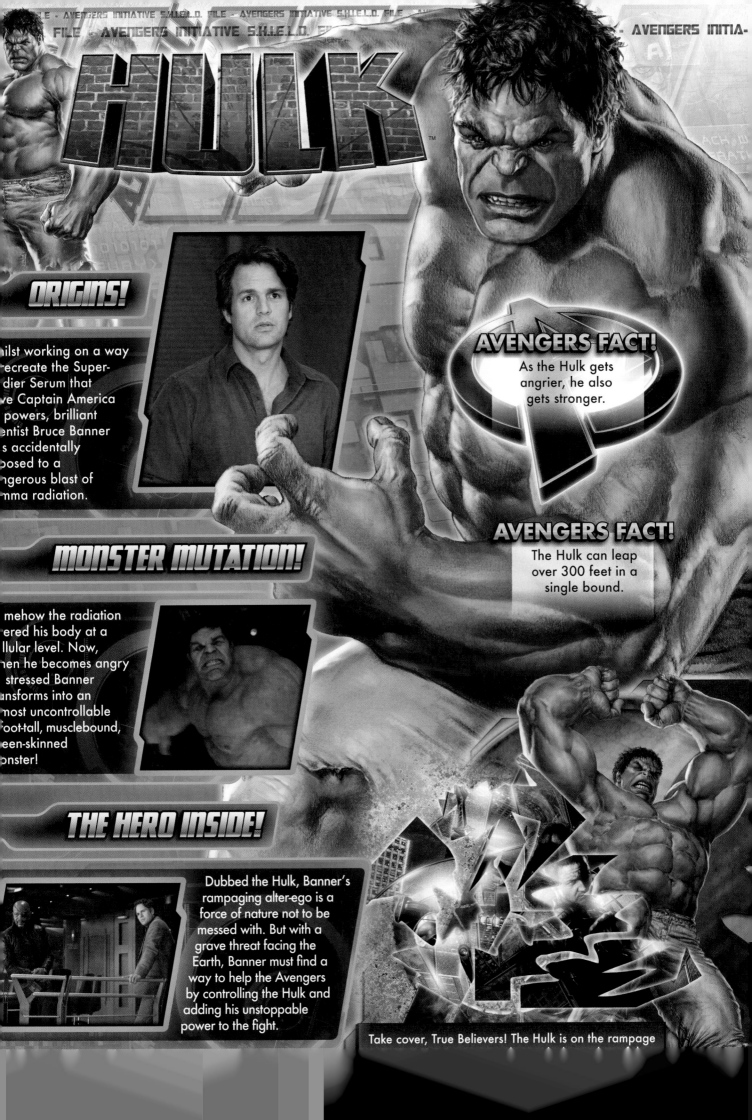

S.H.I.E.L.D.

To be a S.H.I.E.L.D. operative you need to be stronger than a Navy SEAL, more stealthy than a Secret Service Agent and smarter than a college Professor. **See if you've got the right stuff by solving these puzzles - ace the test and we might even give you a try-out for the Avengers!**

HIDDEN HEROES!

Being a S.H.I.E.L.D. Agent means you have the absolute best tech at your disposal. Using these state of the art night vision goggles see if you can spot which 4 members of the Avengers are hiding in the shadows.

TARGET LOCKED ---- MAG X 10

A
B
C
D

A
B
C
D

CODE BREAKER!

Test your espionage skills by using the code key below to crack these passwords and access these ultra-secure files.

FILE:
BRUCE BANNER
PASSWORD:

FILE:
AVENGERS INITIATIVE
PASSWORD:

FILE:
QUINJET
PASSWORD:

FILE:
TESSERACT
PASSWORD:

A B C D E F G H I J K L M N O P Q R S T U V W X Y Z

GRIDLOCK!

Somewhere in this grid are all the names of the Avengers. Can you work out where they are all hiding?

Bonus Test: One of the names appears twice. See if you can spot it!

```
U B T H O R S G W K G P E J
S H Z L W C X O E L D M Y E
Y U C R I R O N M A N W S Y
P L T O W Q Z M F B N C O E
M K C B Y I K O P S A Z W K
W U Y O B L A C K W I D O W
C A P T A I N A M E R I C A
A G H W C N I H U L K W O H
```

IRON MAN ✓   THOR ☐   HULK ☐

CAPTAIN AMERICA ☐   BLACK WIDOW ☐

HAWKEYE ☐   BONUS TEST ☐

SEEING DOUBLE!

Take a look at these two pictures of the Avengers in action. See if you can spot the 8 differences!

☐ ☐ ☐ ☐ ☐ ☐ ☐

S.H.I.E.L.D.

Answering only to the World Security Council, the Strategic Homeland Intervention, Enforcement and Logistics Division is a global taskforce dedicated to protecting the planet from danger.

Specially recruited from all over the world, S.H.I.E.L.D. Agents are handpicked from the very best soldiers, spies and intelligence operatives. They receive the very best training and have access to some of the most hi-tech equipment available.

NICK FURY

As the Director of S.H.I.E.L.D. it's Nick Fury's responsibility to make sure the world stays safe. From the bridge of S.H.I.E.L.D.'s mobile command centre, the Helicarrier, Fury can keep tabs on global events and instantly deploy his forces to wherever they are needed.

Realising that the world now faces dangers unlike any it's endured before, Fury has put together a dossier of superhumans known as the 'Avengers Initiative'. If a global-scale threat occurs, Fury intends to assemble these heroes into an elite defensive force.

REVEALED!

AGENT COULSON

Agent Phil Coulson has been Nick Fury's eyes and ears over the last few years, keeping tabs on heroes such as Thor, Iron Man and the Hulk. Despite the amazing things he's seen, Agent Coulson always remains levelheaded and is famed for his icy calm when under pressure.

S.H.I.E.L.D. FACT!

He might not look it, but Agent Coulson is a highly skilled martial artist and has lightning fast combat reflexes that would put a Navy SEAL to shame.

S.H.I.E.L.D. FACT!

Agent Coulson is a huge fan of Captain America and even has a complete collection of Captain America trading cards!

MARIA HILL

Maria Hill is Nick Fury's right-hand woman. Though she might not always agree with some of Fury's ideas, especially when it comes to the Avengers Initiative, she is fiercely loyal to him.

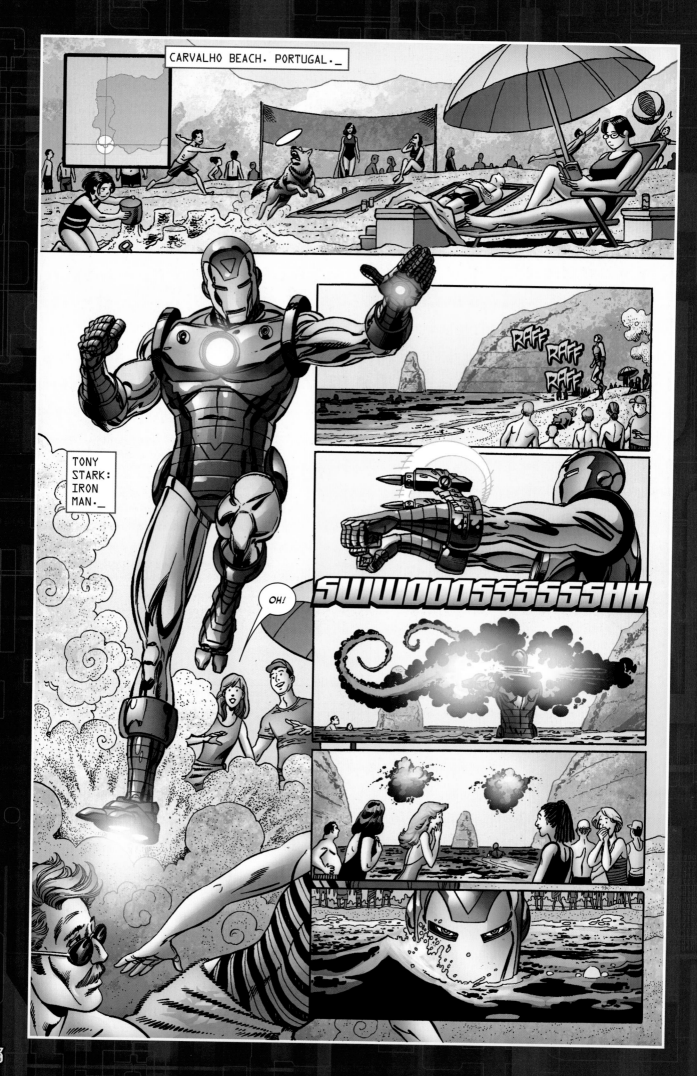

PIRATES OF DEEP WATER!

WRITER: PAUL TOBIN
PENCILS/LAYOUTS: RONAN CLIQUET DE OLIVEIRA
INKS / FINISHES: AMILTON SANTOS
LETTERS: DAVID SHARPE

COLOURS: SOTOCOLOR
EDITOR: NATHAN COSBY
ASSISTANT EDITOR: MICHAEL HORWITZ
REPRINT EDITOR: ED HAMMOND

AY, YOU BIG
TAL BABY!
STAY AWAY
FROM THE
GIRL!

PLAY NICE!
PLAY NICE!

WHERE'S YOUR
ARMING SWITCH? TONY
WANTS TO MAKE YOU GO
BACK TO SLEEP!

HERE YOU
ARE! AND NOW
I JUST--

CONTINUED ON PAGE 47

IRON MAN

SUIT UP!

...ionaire businessman
...d genius inventor
...ny Stark is the
...ator of the Iron
...an armour - an
...redible hi-tech
...ttle suit with
...ough power to
...rns its pilot into
...ne-man army.

NEW & IMPROVED!

...ny created the original
...mour in order to free
...mself from a terrorist
...oup who had kidnapped
...m. Since then, he has
...odified the design many
...mes, adding new features
...d upgrading core
...ystems. His current armour
...the Iron Man Mark VI.

ARMOURED AVENGER!

Though Tony Stark can
sometimes be incredibly
reckless, he's takes his
responsibility as Iron Man
very seriously. When Nick
Fury needs to assemble the
Avengers, he knows that
Iron Man will be ready to
answer the call - no matter
how dangerous the mission!

AVENGERS FACT!
Each glove is fitted with a
palm-mounted flight-stabiliser
that can fire a super-charged
repulsor blast

AVENGERS FACT!
Iron Man can fly at speeds
that can easily break the
sound barrier!

Help Iron Man crack open these top secret
S.H.I.E.L.D. files by spotting the one access switch
that DOESN'T have a red switch next to it.

S.H.I.E.L.D. DATA CORE ACCESS >>>>>

A B C D E F G H

1 2 3 4 5 6 7 8 9 10

43

The Avengers are ready for action but they still need a splash of colour to save the world in style! So grab your pens or pencils and finish off these pictures of the world's mightiest heroes!

ARTISTS

CAPTAIN AMERICA

IRON MAN

HULK

ASSEMBLE

BLACK WIDOW

HAWKEYE

THOR

BLACK WIDOW

BEST OF THE BEST!

When it comes to covert missions no other S.H.I.E.L.D. operative even comes close to the Black Widow. She is without doubt the world's greatest espionage agent and has turned spying into an art form.

SPY GAMES!

Breaking into high-security buildings, surveillance work and infiltrating criminal organisations are all in a days work for Natasha Romanoff. Nick Fury knows that he can always rely on her to get the job done, making her the perfect candidate for the Avengers initiative.

TEAMWORK!

In the past, Natasha has teamed up many times with fellow S.H.I.E.L.D. Agent Hawkeye and the two have developed a close bond of friendship. If Clint was ever in trouble, there is nothing Natasha wouldn't do to ensure his safety.

AVENGERS FACT!

Her bracelets contain a miniature 'Widow's Sting' energy blaster.

START

The Black Widow needs to infiltrate this secret base without setting off any alarms. Can you work out which way she should go to avoid the sensors?

FINISH

TEN MILES OFF THE COAST OF PORTUGAL.—

SO, NATASHA, ALLOW ME TO SAVE YOU MANY QUESTIONS.

I AM ZOYA SIDOROV. THE **WHITE SPIDER.**

I'VE HEARD OF YOU. SUPPOSED TO BE MY *REPLACEMENT.* I THINK THAT MAKES YOU MY *THIRTY-EIGHTH* "REPLACEMENT," AND YET, HERE I *STILL* AM.

I LIKE THAT YOU *KICK.* I WOULD NOT WANT YOU TO BE *BORING.*

NOW PLEASE, WHAT *ELSE* DO YOU THINK YOU KNOW ABOUT ME?

REPORTEDLY IN CHARGE OF *DEEP WATER,* A CRIMINAL ASSOCIATION DEVOTED TO THE OVERTHROW OF THE RUSSIAN GOVERNMENT, FUNDED BY *ADVANCED IDEA MECHANICS,* ANOTHER CRIMINAL ORGANIZATION.

CRIMINALS ARE ONLY CRIMINALS *UNTIL* THEY COME OUT ON *TOP.* A FACT THAT *YOU* SHOULD EMBRACE, CONSIDERING YOUR *LIVELY* PAST.

THE NAME *DEEP WATER,* DOES IT HAVE ANYTHING TO DO WITH THIS BIG UGLY HUNK OF UNDER-WATER METAL?

WHY, *YES.* IT HAS *EVERYTHING* TO DO WITH IT. I THOUGHT YOU *KNEW.*

THIS *IS* DEEP WATER.

TONY!

YOU WILL *PARDON* THE *COMMON CLOTHES* IN WHICH YOU AWOKE, BUT IF *YOU* ARE LIKE *ME*, YOU HAD MANY HIDDEN WEAPONS AND TOOLS.

AND SO, I HAVE TAKEN NO CHANCES.

GOODBYE, NATASHA.

UNFFF!

SSSKLANNGG

ACTUALLY, IF YOU WERE LIKE ME--

--YOU WOULD HAVE *STOLEN* A *LOCKPICK* FROM THE *WHITE SPIDER.*

KLIKKTT

KTUTT

AND YOU WOULD HAVE *TONY STARK* DOING YOUR *FINGERNAILS.*

STATION ANOTHER *SHOCK TEAM* IN FRONT OF *IRON MAN'S* CELL!

NOW!

YOU TWO! COME WITH ME!

BUT-- IRON MAN'S CELL IS--

THE BLACK WIDOW CAN'T *POSSIBLY* BELIEVE SHE CAN FREE *IRON MAN,* AND *THAT* MEANS THAT SHE IS CREATING A *DIVERSION!*

WE NEED TO DISCOVER HER *TRUE* OBJECTIVE!

WHITE SPIDER. *THERE* YOU ARE.

WELCOME TO MY *WEB.*

...AND LET THE **MONSTERS** SEE WHERE THEY ARE.

CONTINUED ON PAGE 57

MEET THE NEXT AVENGER...
YOU!

By now you must be an Avengers expert, so it's about time you joined the ranks of Earth's Mightiest Heroes! Grab your pens and pencils and sketch below what you'd look like if YOU were a member of the Avengers team.

Make sure you fill in your codename along with any amazing powers, incredible skills or special weapons you might have.

AVENGERS INITIATIVE
NEW RECRUIT

FILE: AVE091963

CODENAME:

POWERS/ABILITIES:

SKILLS:

WEAPONS:

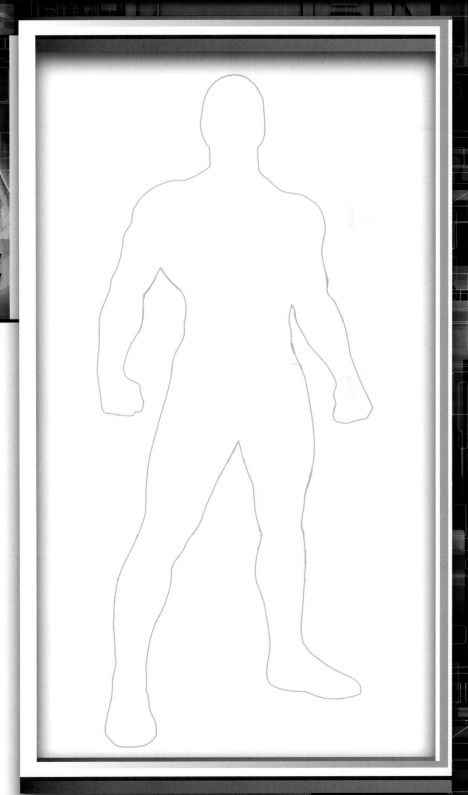

THE QUINJET

When the Avengers assemble, S.H.I.E.L.D. has to guarantee they can get to where they're needed fast. Luckily, they have **the Quinjet** - possibly the most advanced combat/transport jet on the planet!

The turbojet engines can reach speeds of Mach 2.1.

Though it's a tight squeeze, the Quinjet has enough cargo space to carry all of the Avengers.

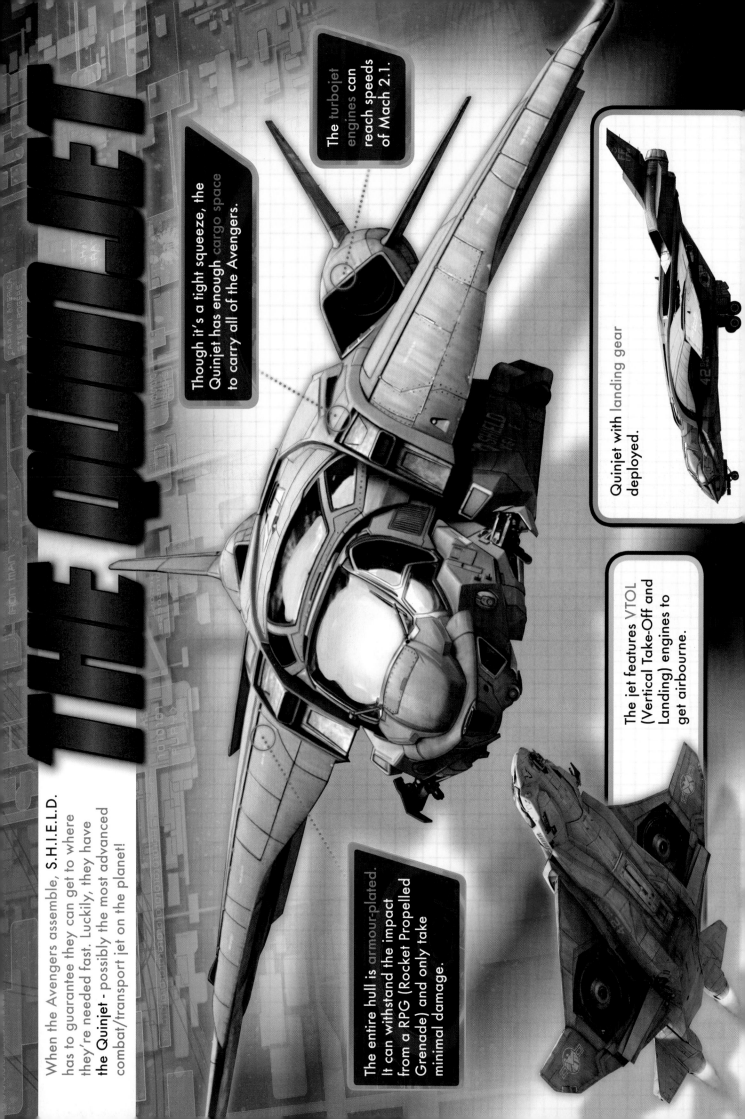

Quinjet with landing gear deployed.

The jet features VTOL (Vertical Take-Off and Landing) engines to get airbourne.

The entire hull is armour-plated. It can withstand the impact from a RPG (Rocket Propelled Grenade) and only take minimal damage.

MISSION DEBRIEF

Listen up, recruits. We've got an important mission that's going to test your memory skills like never before. See if you can answer these questions on the two adventure strips from this annual without looking back through the comic pages. Good luck!

ONCE AND FUTURE AVENGERS!

1 At the start of the strip, what had Loki stolen from Merlin?

A. His belt
B. His boots
C. His beard

2 Which famous King did Thor and Captain America meet in the comic?

A. King Edward
B. King Arthur
C. King Kong

3 How many heads did the dragon have that the two heroes fought?

A. 2   **B.** 4   **C.** 8

PIRATES OF DEEP WATER!

4 What was the White Spider's real name?

A. Zoya Spidorov
B. Rita Arachnea
C. Olga Scoprius

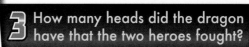

5 Why couldn't Iron Man's armour detect the Deep Water satellite?

A. It was hidden in a cave
B. It had a cloaking device
C. His suit's scanning equipment had gone rusty

6 Take a look at this scene and see if you can spot the 4 differences.

HOW DID YOU DO? CHECK THE ANSWERS ON PAGE 62 TO SEE HOW MANY YOU'VE GOT RIGHT!

ANSWERS

11 Captain America – VIBRANIUM

12 Thor - D is the correct match

22 Hawkeye – Total score: 100

31 Hulk – The picture is of Hawkeye

43 Iron Man – Button D6

46 Black Widow

32 S.H.I.E.L.D. Agent Training

Hidden Heroes: Hawkeye, Thor, Iron Man and Captain America

Code Breaker: Avengers Initiative - ASSEMBLE, Quinjet - FLIGHT, Tesseract - ASGARD, Bruce Banner – GAMMA.

Gridlocked:

Seeing Double: Purple Hulk, Hawkeye's missing quiver, A on Cap's mask, Strap on Thor's hammer, Black Widow's hair, Iron Man's eyes, discs on Thor's costume & Iron Man's shoulder plating.

61 Mission Debrief – 1 – A, 2 – B, 3 – B, 4 – A, 5 – B, 6